50 Things to Know Book Series
Reviews from Readers

Great achievable advice written in everyday language. Suitable for all stages of life. Spot on recognizing and addressing the self limiting behaviors we all have. Joe P.

50 THINGS TO KNOW ABOUT HEALTHY HABITS

Change the Destructive to Constructive

Christina Fanelli

50 Things to Know About Habits Copyright © 2020 by
CZYK Publishing LLC.
All Rights Reserved.

All rights reserved. No part of this book may be reproduced in any form or by any electronic or mechanical means including information storage and retrieval systems, without permission in writing from the author. The only exception is by a reviewer, who may quote short excerpts in a review. The statements in this book are of the authors and may not be the views of CZYK Publishing or 50 Things to Know.

Cover designed by: Ivana Stamenkovic
Cover Image: https://pixabay.com/photos/raise-challenge-landscape-mountain-3338589/

CZYK Publishing Since 2011.

50 Things to Know

Lock Haven, PA
All rights reserved.
ISBN: 9798557744157

50 THINGS TO KNOW ABOUT HABITS

BOOK DESCRIPTION

Do you have habits? Are they bad habits?

Are they good habits for you, but bad habits for others? If you answered yes to any of these questions then this book is for you...

50 Things to Know About Habits by author Christina Fanelli offers an approach to work on your habits. Although there's nothing wrong with some habits, based on knowledge from the world's leading experts and others in what one perceives as a good habit others may not.

In these pages, you'll discover if what you think is a good habit is good or could it be better. If it's a bad habit, how to change it, or why it should be changed. This book will help you break habits that are destructive to you or others and make you happy with yourself.

By the time you finish this book, you will know what you have been doing that others find as bad habits that you have…. So grab YOUR copy today. You'll be glad you did.

TABLE OF CONTENTS

6. GOAL ENHANCERS – GOOD HABITS
GOAL STOPPERS – BAD HABITS
FIX THE BAD HABIT –
PRODUCTIVE GOAL ENHANCEMENTS

7. PHYSICAL – GOOD HABITS
PHYSICAL – BAD HABITS
FIX THE BAD HABIT –
PRODUCTIVE PHYSICAL PLANNING

8. MENTAL – GOOD HABITS
MENTAL – BAD HABITS
FIX THE BAD HABIT –
PRODUCTIVE MENTAL ENHANCING

9. GENERATIONAL - GOOD HABITS
18. GENERATIONAL - BAD HABITS
FIX THE BAD HABIT –
PRODUCTIVE GENERATIONAL PLANNING

10. TELEVISION INFLUENCED - GOOD HABITS
TELEVISION INFLUENCED - BAD HABITS
FIX THE BAD HABIT –
PRODUCTIVE TELEVISION PLANNING

11. PEER PRESSURE – GOOD HABITS
PEER PRESSURE –
BAD HABITS
FIX THE BAD HABIT –
PEER PRESSURE PLANNING

11. NON-JUDGEMENTAL – GOOD HABITS
JUDGEMENTAL – BAD HABITS
FIX THE BAD HABIT –
NON-JUDGMENTAL PLANNING

12. COOKING - GOOD HABITS
COOKING – BAD HABITS
FIX THE BAD HABIT –
COOKING PLANNING

13. EATING – GOOD HABITS
EATING – BAD HABITS
FIX THE BAD HABIT –
EATING PLANNING

14. ALCOHOL GOOD HABITS
ALCOHOL BAD HABITS
FIX THE BAD HABIT – ALCOHOL PLANNING

15. GAMBLING GOOD HABITS
GAMBLING - BAD HABITS
FIX THE BAD HABIT –
GAMBLING PLANNING

16. EXERCISING GOOD HABITS
EXERCISING BAD HABITS
FIX THE BAD HABIT –
EXERCISING ENHANCING

17. CLEANING GOOD HABITS
CLEANING BAD HABITS
FIX THE BAD HABIT –
CLEANING PLANNING

18. AFTER WORK – GOOD HABITS
AFTER WORK – BAD HABITS
FIX THE BAD HABIT –
AFTER WORK PLANNING

19. LEISURE TIME – GOOD HABITS
LEISURE TIME – BAD HABITS
FIX THE BAD HABIT –
LEISURE TIME PLANNING

20. DRUGS – GOOD HABITS
DRUGS – BAD HABITS
FIX THE BAD HABIT –
DRUG USAGE PLANNING

21. TRAVELING – GOOD HABITS
TRAVELING – BAD HABITS
FIX THE BAD HABIT –
TRAVEL PLANNING

22. SELF - DETERMINATION –
GOOD HABITS
SELF – DETERMINATION –
BAD HABITS
FIX THE BAD HABIT –
SELF DETERMINATION ENHANCING

23. HANDLING ISSUES GOOD HABITS
HANDLING ISSUES – BAD HABITS
FIX THE BAD HABIT -
HANDLING ISSUES PLANNING

24. OPTIMISTIC DISPOSITION – GOOD HABIT
PESSIMISTIC DISPOSITION – BAD HABIT
FIX THE BAD HABIT – OPTIMISTIC
    DISPOSITION ENHANCING

25. BRAGGING – DOMINANCE IN
    CONVERSATIONS
FIX THE BAD HABIT - STOPPING BRAGGING
    PLANNING

DEEP BREATHING – GOOD HABIT PLANNING
ASSUMING – BAD HABIT
FIX THE BAD HABIT - STOPPING ASSUMING
    PLANNING
References:

DEDICATION

To my close family members, my kids Miranda and William Green III that show I have been a successful single parent. To Scott Congdon and his kids that showed me I can be included in another family's life. Both of these insights have helped me overcome my bad habit of not having faith in myself.

ABOUT THE AUTHOR

My name is Christina; I come from what used to be a very prosperous city, Elmira, New York. I work in a healthcare setting now and have worked in the education field both as an Administrative Assistant and as an Instructor. This advancement in employment came along with my continuing education while being a single parent of two wonderful children that are now grown and on their own. Through all of this, I have had different habits. Some that I was forced to acquire to be able to succeed with a job, school, and kids, and some that I acquired that I had to change along the way.

This is my third writing to share my education, research, and experiences. My other publications can be found on my Amazon Author Page and I also can be found on Facebook, Twitter, LinkedIn, and I do have a Freelance Copywriter website.

"First we form habits. Then they form us."

- Jim Rohn

hat is a habit? It is something that is done repetitively. It can be something that is done by choice, by what was taught, by force, and sometimes there is a habit that is not even known. People may not even know that they have a habit, but become informed of their habits by others and react.

There are conscious and subconscious habits. A habit can have different kinds of ending results.

- It can be a good habit and have positive results
- It can be a bad habit and have negative results
- It can be an ugly habit that impacts others
- It can be a destructive habit
- It can be a constructive habit
- It can be a habit of something that is learned on purpose as a habit
- It can be a medically forced habit (bath, teeth)
- Sometimes we don't even know it that we are doing a habit (social media, email)
- Sometimes we even get forced to break or acquire habits, do not hug and wear face masks in public in 2020

Taking a look into the different types of habits that there are and how they come about will give you a better understanding of them. They will help you change the bad habits or the habits that you want to change, enhance the habits you want to keep, see the habits you have that you are not aware of, and make some constructive changes to a happier, healthier you!

This should be a learning experience. There are good habits and bad habits that are listed to share with explanations and some examples. Then there is a Fix the Bad Habit that will give suggestions and recommendations on how to stop, fix, or improve that bad habit. For each subject, these are not the only good or bad habits and these are not the only fixes. If you are instigated to note another good, bad, or fix from any of these, that's even better. Feel free to share and them with me and we can add them for others on my author page.

1. ROUTINES- GOOD HABITS

Everyone knows what a routine is, but not everyone has a routine that they maintain. It is a form of a pattern for accomplishment; it helps create the structure for home, life, for raising children, and just about anything. These routines for families can include the daily schedule of homework, dinner, shower, then television, or game time.

Reading is a good routine to start. If it can be started with children at bedtime at a young age, not only does it stimulate their mind, but helps them to form a routine habit that will help them sleep better. There are no limitations on what kind of learning they will acquire, but the options of the different types of literature are limitless.

ROUTINES- BAD HABITS

Some routines can be bad habits and start very young. However, some routines can stifle creativity if it is too strict. In today's society, it is easy to spend a lot of money and not even notice. People like to shop and look around for a deal or just for enjoyment. However, if they find what they are looking for or find a sale or deal on an item that seems unbelievable, they tend to over-purchase.

Routines also get us to forget the value of what we do and why and we still do what is no longer necessary. Take for instance things for children. They start as infants and we do everything for them. Unless we stop and look at them, we are still doing everything for them like cleaning their room for them, when they should learn to not make a mess or not having them help with things that at one time they were too young, but now the could like mowing the yard and shoveling. We also get so accustomed to the smoothness of routines, that when something unusual happens or an emergency arises, we cannot handle it.

FIX THE BAD HABIT-
PRODUCTIVE ROUTINES

Having routines makes us more efficient at home and in other scenarios. It gives us structure so that we have less to think and plan for, but still accomplish. This gives us extra time to plan for more valuable things like reading and that can make learning easier throughout life. If started at a young age it is known more as entertainment and later when it is necessary for school or employment it doesn't seem like additional work.

Spending money can be costly in time with family, space for purchases, and finances. It can affect the lives of all the individuals that are within the income and space when money is being spent and cause it to appear to be greed and cause resentment.

Routine habits will have effects now and possibly even more so in the future. Kids will not know how to do common everyday things like laundry if we don't stop and look at our routine and modify it to teach them how to do it. Therefore, when it comes to a routine that is a necessity or is bad like spending money, only do it when necessary. Stick to routines that stimulate growth in you, your family, and your life. It will help reduce your procrastination, build momentum, and give you self-confidence, but don't let it become your life so that you get upset when you don't finish it.

2. PLANNING- GOOD HABITS

Planning can be a very advantageous action. When there is an event or a project that will be completed or is needed, planning is great. It allows thinking about what all the event or project requires, needs, or wants. It allows for changes and alterations to be made based on demands to be met long before needed. This allows for the outcome to be more as desired in a less stressed, tight schedule with a smaller chance of the requests and demands not being met. That is because if what is requested cannot be met one way if planned there is time to make changes and do it another way. In the end, the results are what is desired, with giving a word or contract the work is finished, and the stress for completion and perfection has a better chance of being met.

It is also found that if you plan you do not miss things or opportunities. An example is going on a trip but without plans. You get up in the morning at the motel and start looking for the day's plans and then in a blink of an eye notice that it's dinner time. Have a plan for the day at least the night before so you have time to figure out what you want to do, how, and when so you do not miss anything that day.

PLANNING- BAD HABITS

It does not happen very often, but it does happen that what is planned for changes or gets canceled. Take for example a job proposal that you received. You propose and submit your quote and are so excited that you tell the staff about it, start planning the schedules, purchasing supplies….and then you find out the customer has given the project to competition. Now you have to go back and be the bearer of bad news to the employees, take down the schedule, and return any supplies that were purchased only for this project.

It can also be that too much time is spent planning and then it never gets started or passes the due date for submittal. How about planning that is done without all the information. How about the planning that is done for others and then they do not follow it. They may get the plans, but they do not follow it or find that it is missing information because of a lack of information.

FIX THE BAD HABIT –
PRODUCTIVE PLANNING

When it comes to planning, changes that are requested or demanded can be adjusted or reconfigured to make for the best results possible if done with all the information in a timely and economical manner. If the planning is not handled properly it can result in being costly in time, finances, and results. Therefore, until you have the full power of the project and the contributors don't proceed with the plans.

Keep working on the stability projects and planning for the next project to bid on. Get as much information as possible when planning for others. Plan, but do not proceed to purchase until acceptance has been received

3. HOBBIES- GOOD HABITS

A hobby can be a good habit to have. It can improve your life by its benefits to health mentally, physically, or even by its worth. Reading is a great hobby. It doesn't matter if it is on a kindle or an actual book. The options that reading gives you are limitless. Take for example it could help your style of cooking. It can be helpful if you don't know much about cooking because you will learn to make food that is better for consumption and your wallet.

Hobbies are usually something that a person does that they enjoy. Knitting is an example of a good habit. It is a productive hobby that creates different items such as hats, sweaters, blankets, etc. from yarn. This is a hobby that relaxes the mind and body while doing something that creates something positive.

HOBBIES – BAD HABITS

Although playing also seems like a relaxing enjoyable hobby, it can be addicting and unproductive. Video games can be fun and they can become a hobby, but they can be addicting. The games can be so much fun and challenging that it is very difficult to stop playing. This can cause a loss of time perspective and a lot of needed activities to not be completed. There is also social media that becomes a habit. It causes a feeling of it being a requirement to participate. Both of these can become addicting and cause a lack of sleep or social withdrawal which has negative results, especially if long term.

FIX THE BAD HABIT –
PRODUCTIVE HOBBIES

The repetition of a hobby can impact lives. If it is a positive, productive hobby, it can give a relaxing impact on the mind and body of everyone within its vicinity. However, if the hobby is addicting and causes other things to be put aside or not be completed then it can have a bad impact on everyone's life. Therefore, if there is a hobby and it is one that is done for entertainment and is desired to be continued, set a time and a time limit for it. So if it is playing video games, don't let yourself start the game until all the necessary activities are done first, or set a time limit on the activity, and stick to it. Keep hobbies both the good and the bad in moderation so that they do not become an obsession.

4. HEALTHY – GOOD HABITS

Trying to keep yourself and your family healthy is a good habit to have. Planning a menu for the week before shopping can help you keep the food within the home healthy. Take the time to decide what meals are going to be prepared for dinner each night and what food is necessary for lunches and then include what food and supplies are now low and add them to the list. There are healthy menus and recipes available on the internet for any restrictions such as diabetes or peanut allergies. Only pick up what is on the list. This will keep healthy food in the home.

Standing up and walking regularly helps the body consume fats and sugars that cause health problems. When the weather is nice, go and use some muscles that don't get used regularly. Stretch to get good circulation before and after exercising and always be in proper posture

UNHEALTHY – BAD HABITS

There are habits that people acquire over the years that are not good for their health. Some peeople do not realize that the habits are doing damage to their health and can have a long term effect.

One of the most popular, but least thought about is the lack of consumption of water. We think of energy drinks and soda, but not water. The lack of water can cause problems with bowels, optimal muscles, and the aging of skin.

Eating late or just before bed can cause indigestion and cause problems sleeping. While the body is trying to digest, sleep stays afar and it enhances restlessness. Thus causing the body to not getting enough sleep, which can impact the body both mentally and physically. The lack of sleep affects the immunity system, judgment, heart health and contributes to depression.

Some bad health habits are also obtained due to peer pressure or from watching others. An example of this is smoking or vaping. In today's society, it is very common to see people start smoking or vaping even though they are known to be addictive and unhealthy. This is common among youth from peer pressure or media. These habits are acquired and now have even caused some legalities.

FIX THE BAD HABIT – HEALTHY PLANNING

Keeping healthy is a high priority in today's society. Bulletin boards, television commercials, even multi-media advertising all show healthy planning and great physical appearances.

When looking at food, goods, services, advertisements, recipes, or even commercials the health information is noted somewhere. That is so that when people are looking at a good or service and trying to keep healthy they can find the information to see that it meets their standard of health. However, when it comes to something being unhealthy it tends to be in small print, said quickly so not really heard, or not even mentioned.

When out in public there are designated areas for individuals that are doing something that is considered unhealthy such as smoking or vaping. Therefore, if you are thinking of or have already started something that is an unhealthy habit like smoking, vaping, or eating unhealthy or try to stop now. If you need help, there are ways to get help from a medical professional.

Keeping small amounts of activity and watching consumption can change your health from bad to good. Exercising regularly gives more energy and lowers health risks like breast and prostate cancer.

5. FAMILY – GOOD HABITS

Having a family to enjoy is one of the greatest parts of life. It is one of the times that we get to be around the people that we love, enjoy, and grow with throughout our entire lives. Schedules sound like more work and they are in the beginning, but they will save time in the end. They become a routine and that helps keep things that need to be done, completed. Here are some to think about doing yourself if you don't already or some to get your children to start to help them in better development. Make your bed in the morning, it shows neatness and gives you time start waking up, some exercise, and starts the routine mode. Wash your hands and face to get clean, refreshed, and regularly and just before certain chores with your hands like cooking, sitting down to eat dinner, or setting the table.

A good habit to have with family is to have dinner together on a regular basis and to make it special family time. In today's world having time together without distractions such as Televisions, radios, and cell phones is a challenge.

One good family habit is to have everyone come together at the dinner table as often as possible and have dinner together at the table without the television and radio on and without cell phones. Take this opportunity to tell how each person's day went. Have everyone tell the good part of their day, then the bad part of their day, and a weird part of the day if it exists for humor.

This gives parents an awareness of what is going on in their children's lives, the opportunity to give advice on situations, and to be aware of circumstances as they arise.

This also gives the adults a chance to share how life is in the adult, in the working world, and bring up subjects that are harder to find an excuse to bring up otherwise.

FAMILY – BAD HABITS

When kids are young they are in the state of developing. They are becoming and they can be molded to be what they will be when they are an adult. They do as they see others do. This is a parent's opportunity to shape the child. One of the most important habits is to teach them at a young age is respect. Please and thank you, tone of voice, facial expressions, and choice of words have an impact as much or more than the subject matter of the conversation..

There are also many things that we do not realize. With busy schedules, fast food tends to be used more than it should be and it is not healthy. Not only does it become a habit to do around the busy schedule, but the kids start to expect it. It is hard to think differently after you have been a teenager, to a young adult, to a parent, and have done the same. Habits like swearing and sarcastic comments that you acquire need to be broken before your kids pick it up. Talk to them, with them, and around them the way you want them to talk, respectful.

Children need to know that they need to learn, that they do not know everything. They need parents, that they need to grow and mature in a positive constructive way and that their parents are helping them. When a child is not respectful to an adult, what the adult says to do means nothing. It is the same for everyone else in that child's life because they know they can and they don't have respect for anyone, but themselves.

FIX THE BAD HABIT –
PRODUCTIVE FAMILY PLANNING

The family is the molder of each individual. When two adults come together to develop a family there is a greater perspective on families because of the different upbringings that each adult had. If a disagreement happens within the home, be respectful of your body language and your voice.

Get all the family members on a schedule. It is the best way to know and inform a family. It also makes open communication a priority for family and it leaves opportunity for discussion. However, a disrespectful child will do what they want, talkbacks, not follow the rules, and eventually are mean to the parents and everyone else. Take the opportunity of youth to mold kids to know that life is an adventure and you never know what it's going to throw at you. Adults are there for you, but only if you're respectful, otherwise, you're on your own. Try to keep communication a top priority throw in the question of anyone having anything funny or humorous in their day, just to have the opportunity to share the entertaining parts of life, it is what you make of it.

Evening schedules can be busy so plan ahead for dinner instead of stopping at a fast-food restaurant for something quick. Make dinner in the crockpot so it is ready when you get home or pack sandwiches that can be grabbed and thrown into the cooler.

Teach kids young to be conservative, buy the kids water bottles that can be washed and refilled. Then they will know that they do not have to spend money o water bottles at the store every time they go out. Also, have them clean and put away their sports equipment when they are done with it so they understand it does not need to be replaced as quickly.

6. GOAL ENHANCERS – GOOD HABITS

It is sometimes so hard to accomplish anything, even a daily schedule, let alone a long-term goal. One way to accomplish a goal is to make it short-term and give yourself a bonus once it is accomplished. If it is a long-term goal break it down into steps and once each step is accomplished give yourself a bonus. So if you want to have your house cleaned, give yourself a time to have it done and if it is done by that time you give yourself a bubble bath, a glass of wine, watch a movie, order dinner delivery, etc. If it is a long term goal like remodeling the living room, set a goal for each part of the project. In the first week write out all the parts to accomplish (paint, carpet, new furniture, etc.) and put them in the order to do them. Next week, purchase the supplies needed for the project (patching, primer, and paint) then remove all the wall hangings and fix the holes with the patching, etc. continue creating the small steps to achieve each week and after the step is achieved, give yourself the bonus.

GOAL STOPPERS – BAD HABITS

We tend to be our own worst hypocrites and want things to be perfect. This tends to be one of the desires within us, which holds us back from achieving goals of all shapes and sizes. It is hard to watch others accomplish something and not feel like you should have done that or been able to do that yourself. In today's world with directions, information, and suggestions being at your fingertips on the internet it is easy to be a hypocrite. I can do better than them, but then never try or I will do it because it's so expensive to pay someone else to do it, but then don't do it because it's too much work.

We also tend to fear failure. Sometimes it feels like a failure to yourself and that would be a failure that shows you're worth even less. Then there are always excuses that are self-justification, but stop advancement towards the goal. Therefore, the goal still doesn't get accomplished.

FIX THE BAD HABIT – PRODUCTIVE GOAL ENHANCEMENTS

Completion of goals can make for a productive happier life. However, there are both long-term and short-term goals and each can cause different kinds of set-backs. If you have short term goals, set up a reward or gift for yourself once the accomplishment is made. If it's a long-term goal, break it down into smaller individualized goals and expectations that can be accomplished and so you can feel like you are making progress and still receive the accomplishment bonuses. Keep giving yourself the bonus to feel the accomplishment, fulfillment, and to thank you.   Don't procrastinate or set the goals too high, it causes the desire to see distractions to steer off track and lose consistency.

Today people think it is so easy to do anything, but they do not want to do anything themselves, it is just easier to complain about not being done or about how things are done. To stop this habit, remember it's only you that can do anything about the goal, whether it is doing the work yourself or finding someone else to do it with you or for you. So don't let the work not be done and complain, set a short-term goal for you to do it, or to find someone to do it for you.

7. PHYSICAL – GOOD HABITS

Physical health is important to be happy. When a person feels healthy, they find it easier to be happy. When people hear the words physical and exercise some think of work out gyms, but that is not necessary. The habit of a couple walks a week, bike rides or even deep breathing can be a form of exercise that is good for physical health. Elevation of the heart rate each day for 20 minutes just by walking briskly outside while hydrating with water can do immense physical improvements. Not only are you helping your cognitive functions and relieving stress with nature, but you can have water or even coffee on this walk and it will count towards your daily water intake.

PHYSICAL – BAD HABITS

In today's society, it is hard to keep up. Not only do we have work and home life, but many of us feel obligated to social media, emails, websites, and more daily. These do not require physical activity and people start to do it out of habit. These activities make it more difficult to find time to sleep. When people do not get enough sleep, it takes a toll on their bodies. Poor posture is common today from hunching over with laptops, cellphones, and game consoles like Xbox and PlayStation. This can cause tension headaches because your 10-pound head is not being properly squared above your shoulders and neck muscles get overworked.

Fingers are in contact with different surfaces all day and night. When it comes to people that have the habit of nail biting, they are putting these germs that are acquired from the surfaces into their mouth.

Yes, for some people nail-biting is a stress reliever, but their are germs from your mouth going to your fingernails can cause infection and inflammation too. It can also damage your jaw with bruxism, which is the grinding or clenching of your teeth and jaw. The American Journal of General Dentistry states it causes facial pain, headaches, tooth sensitivity, and tooth and gum loss.

Take a break from the world and stress, don't nail bit. Contact a friend or take a dog and go for a brisk walk, enjoy nature, and refresh your body and your mind.

FIX THE BAD HABIT –
PRODUCTIVE PHYSICAL PLANNING

The body is reactive. When there are events or actions the body reacts. If it is a constructive event like exercise the body reacts by making you feel better, helping you sleep, and making you feel mentally and physically more refreshed. When the body is not getting enough physically such as sleep, it reacts destructively. It can cause issues with memory, moods, thinking and concentration, blood pressure, immunity, diabetes, weight gain, and more. If you have to go into your email or want to go to social media daily, hop in a treadmill or walk about your living room the entire time you are there. You can feel like you're keeping up with those obligations and still doing for yourself.

Sit and stand properly for your body's sake, it will have effects later, if you don't. Biting nails can occur and not be realized so there are nail polishes available to assist in curbing the urge to bite by tasting bad. Also keeping nail files and clippers nearby many times, the urge to bite, is a catch in the nail. Beautify yourself, there isn't anybody that is more important.

8. MENTAL – GOOD HABITS

The world today is exhausting. It's hard to not worry and have anxiety, which makes it hard to fall asleep. We are cruel to ourselves and our loved ones. Mindfulness is a great way to start controlling your attention and regulating what you focus on. It is a therapeutic technique for focusing awareness on the present moment while acknowledging feelings, thoughts, and body sensations. It will help you avoid depression, anxiety, and other mental issues that come from worrying, self-criticizing, and procrastinating. Different types of meditation are practiced in different cultures to create the desired calmness behind meditation. The most common are mindfulness, spiritual, focused movement, mantra, transcendental, progressive, loving-kindness, and visualization meditation.

Some people can get enough recuperation from sleeping; however, some people have difficulties sleeping. Some suggestions are being in a routine. Relax awake from a certain time of the day on and go to bed at an approximate same time each day. These times should be set for approximately the same time even on the weekends. It will train your body to start to relax and go to sleep when you go to bed.

It may also be uncomfortable to do, but ask others for feedback on your life, both personally and professionally. We all have blind spots and weaknesses that we are not aware of and they could certainly use some work. People may be a little hesitant to criticize, so listen carefully. Some want to help you, but not seem to mean or feel like they are picking a fight. Do this with assertiveness, but don't be rude. Weed through what they say and think about it. If you want to improve badly enough, you will find it.

MENTAL – BAD HABITS

Feeling guilty can be fine, but only if it is for a limited amount of time and is used for growing and learning from it. We are taught young to not take advantage of what we have, such as eat all the food. We are taught you to eat all the food on your plate. We over-eat and then are uncomfortable. We tend to make problems that don't exist or magnify little issues and then penalize ourselves.

We are notorious to get involved in problems that are not ours with social media and smartphones. We do things, see things, or even remember people, things, and events that we regret. Then we think about it or dwell on it and sometimes post it on social media that magnifies it. For some people, this can lead to relying on others to make you happy or feeling worthy and lead to poor sleep because of restless thinking and bad dreams.

Some people are their own worst enemy. This is because they never seem to achieve what they feel they deserve. However, how they rate what they deserve is comparison and these comparison are not fully known for the other party. It can be because of their disposition, their work, their tone, or even their body language. All of these are ways that each person presents and others read the meaning, whether the message is correct or not. Some of this stems from perfectionism. It may start as a healthy habit to achieve goals, but for some people, it becomes more of a distraction, preoccupation that leads to a failure because of too many mistakes.

FIX THE BAD HABIT –
PRODUCTIVE MENTAL ENHANCING

The different types of mindfulness all have the basic same goal, calm and inner harmony. These are accomplished in different practices but they are for the self-altering of consciousness, inner peace, and self-awareness. It is a positive self-calming that lets you relieve stress where self-belittling does exactly the opposite. Self-belittling can make you stress yourself, you can be your critic, and hurt yourself by doing this. It can even cause physical damage such as an ulcer if it is done long enough. Let things go, trust your gut, and just do it. Yes, you may not get the results you want the first couple of times, but you will eventually start to trust yourself and critique yourself less each time which is exactly what you need.

Don't compare yourself to others. What you have or don't have may not seem like much compared to them, but only to you. You have something they don't and they know what that is, but they will not mention that on social media. You have more to give to yourself and that's the part to remember, you live with yourself not them.

9. GENERATIONAL- GOOD HABITS

The lifestyle that a child is brought up around when they are young eventually becomes how they will live their life and bring up their own children. They use what they learned, the family rituals, school, and neighborhood, social media, and the surrounding society to mold who they become. Holidays are a time of the year to celebrate. It can be a holiday that is celebrated by everyone or one that is only celebrated by your family, but it is a time for the family to get together and share their experiences. It lets people see how things are in other family members' lives and the way things are different in other lives even with the same customs and upbringing. These can be like everyone meeting at Christmas and exchanging gifts or having an annual party in the summer to celebrate the family name. It brings different generations together to share stories and learn customs and see how things have changed.

GENERATIONAL- BAD HABITS

A bad habit that has been learned over the last few generations is social media. People now tend to make social media part of their daily schedule, part of their life, and for some part of their family. The problem with this is that social media is not personal, it doesn't know about you, nor does it care about you. It's a chat board and the subjects that are on that board to chat about can be controversial and cause misunderstandings and loss of relationships.

An example of generation changes are in the college years and requirements. Since the 50s college was stressed for youth. To be successful go to college.

College is not the answer for everything to youth, but that has been drilled into the minds of many for a long time and now they are facing the college debt, global marketing, and the robotics that are taking in their field of study.

The younger generations also expect their parents to finance them long after adulthood and some still live with parents at 30. Anything bad that happens is not their fault, so parents have to help them. Some of this comes from getting praise for doing what is expected of them most of their life and they don't have self-expectations to do more. Later in life, they tend to be super-sensitive and politically correct. Now there is also a shortage of apprentices.

FIX THE BAD HABIT – PRODUCTIVE GENERATIONAL PLANNING

Holidays and customs are a time for celebration. Families that unite for these celebrations have close relations and support for each other. What the younger generation can learn from the older generation during these family events is priceless. It is a time to share with family and that is one of the best joys in life. Visiting social media is now a daily event in the younger generations.

What you meant to say and how it was taken is a common issue when it comes to social media. The way a statement was interpreted may not be how it was intended. This can cause a heated discussion or even an argument. The chances of that argument happening if the parties were talking are much less because of the differences in body language and tones. If there is a discussion that is controversial or has many different viewpoints, social media is not a place to discuss it. Face to face time is the best for this type of communication so that there isn't any reason to not understand the intended results from all parties in the discussion.

The younger generations rely on the "American Dream" and other metaphors and it is taking them some time to realize it doesn't work that way. Many went on to college and now have immense debt and there is a shortage of service trades like plumber, electrician, carpenter, etc. Take any criticism and use it to improve. Set your mind to improve yourself so you can move up in the world. Knowing that you are doing better for you, will allow you to fulfill the need to be politically correct and help someone else. Coming outside that box is happening for the young, just slowly.

10. TELEVISION INFLUENCED- GOOD HABITS

If you have a habit of watching television, make it a good habit. If done correctly, television is one of the fastest ways to boost happiness. Part of that is based on what is watched like feel-good shows like the importance of cholesterol screenings. You will feel informed and self-inspired to take care of yourself. It can even stimulate oxytocin, the "love" hormone. Television can also be used as a timer. When you are watching one of your favorite half-hour shows, jump on your exercise bike and ride for that 30-minute work-out while you laugh.

There are plenty of comedies on television. Laughing is one of the best ways to relieve stress. So if you have the habit of watching television or are influenced by television, watch a comedy. It will relieve your stress with a laugh, sometimes they show you what not to do, and give you a break from reality. Some of these comedies have sarcastic antics that can boost creativity and help find solutions to problems because it stimulations complex thinking and minimizes anger. Nature and animals are wondrous for your brain and emotions. The shows about them help us feel charitable and energetic. They are good conversation stimulators with children and give us the boost to donate our time and money to nature and those in need.

TELEVISION INFLUENCED- BAD HABITS

American Academy of Pediatrics (AAP) has raised concerns about child development related to television. Some children have challenges distinguishing the difference between fantasy and reality television. There is also the fact that violence on television does not always show any serious consequences, sex is shown at inappropriate ages, and with unrealistic body images. This doesn't even count how bad habits like alcohol, cigarettes, gambling, and other unhealthy habits are glamorized. Some people have also thought that television could increase their imagination and vocabulary.

Kids that start on television habits young tend to come from homes of low socioeconomic status, single parents, or teenage parenting.   Kids can be frightened by what they see on television or maybe watching the parent show that is inappropriate for the child's age. Don't watch too much news when the kids are around. It can show things you don't want to think about or that affect you, your community, and your loved ones.

Healthy dramas can be watched for a little learning, but keep it at a minimum. They do tend to be realistic based so they do have a dying and serious disease.

FIX THE BAD HABIT – PRODUCTIVE TELEVISION PLANNING

Limit the amount of time and the shows that kids watch. There are child-oriented learning channels that could be used as the background sound some people feel is a necessity. Use those shows for discussion and discuss the content of the programs and commercials. Criticize negative behaviors exhibited and show how commercials are teasers to make viewers want something that is not a necessity. Limit the length of time for television and set the time to be for after homework, exercise time, and chores are completed.

Be in control of your actions, not influenced. Do activities that are physically and mentally enhanced, not passive television. Use the radio instead. It's free, there is a large assortment of styles, music encourages the use of vocal cords, memorization of songs, exercise from active dancing, and allows freedom of expression. Use music as and inspiration and entertainment and watch the television shows that help you grow and learn, not influence you.

11. PEER PRESSURE – GOOD HABITS

Having friends and family that support you and your decisions can be very influential and inspirational. The sense of belonging or being supported by peers can increase self-confidence. Finding peers that have the same interests, attitudes, and hobbies can help with decisions. It's a reinforcement for what may become a challenge. Knowing that you may struggle, but will have support to provide the ambition to continue with anything can make a difference of following through and making best decisions. You can be the one in need of support or you can be the one to provide support. Either way, being involved with a can-do it disposition will make you and everyone around you feel better. Have a wide range of friends and influences from different backgrounds. It will help you learn more about yourself, others, and see from different perspectives.

PEER PRESSURE –
BAD HABITS

Feeling like a loser is very common, is increasing, and should not be. This comes from the increase in social media, the feeling of the need to compete in irrelevant areas like games, and the ease of anonymous bullying. There are activities and behaviors that peers have those others are compelled to join even if they don't agree. Some of these are alcohol, cigarettes, drugs, risk behavior, family and friend distancing, and changing behaviors to fit in. These will have long-term effects so think about them before you get too accustomed to them. As adults, self-esteem suffers and loss of autonomy and control over life entails.

FIX THE BAD HABIT –
PEER PRESSURE PLANNING

Other people can be very influential on you and your decisions. They can impact your character, make you worry about yourself, or miss out on things. When people look at social media they see what others are or are not doing, think of themselves, and compare what they are doing in their life is irrelevant to what you are doing. The circumstances are different, the backgrounds are different, and what part of life they are in is different. There is no comparison. Don't take their critiques seriously and feel that it's that significant to win or fit in. With cell phones, email, and other types of anonymous contacts it is easy to be bullied and feel like the loser. Keep in mind they are the ones that are hiding behind the text or email. They are the one that is hiding their identity to say it. So is that a bully or a chicken? Don't get in the habit of doing things that can have a long-term mental and physical impact on you later.

Be true to yourself and what you want in your future, they probably won't be in it and you will outgrow them. There is always someone besides you to affirm what you value and help you be what is best for you. You have to live with yourself, not them.

11. NON-JUDGEMENTAL – GOOD HABITS

Before a judgment can be made all the information that is available needs to be known. Education that is obtained by listening and researching can help make critical decisions. Be a good listener and get out of the habit of thinking of a reply while they are still providing their information.

If you are given massive readings of education and suggestions, don't skim and remember the confirmations, ask for more time and read the ones that contradict. The suggestions may work, they may not, but they must give an idea of improvement or diversity. When an idea is useful, make sure that it is relevant to the presented challenges, any others it presents are brought up, and that it isn't so narrow that it confines the options.

JUDGEMENTAL – BAD HABITS

Some people make you feel like a loser, but we do it to ourselves too, but sometimes don't realize we do it. Take into consideration things that you could do, but don't because you feel you have a valid reason not to. For example, how about volunteering. A bad judgment is that without money exchange, there isn't a reason.

We do a lot by labeling. Some prime examples are, fat is sloppy, popular is not intelligent. It's a limitation set before opportunity. When we start to feel down, we start to label everyone else by judging them and it becomes a tedious habit. Everything is judged right down to the color of their nail polish and eventually, people see us as miserable people and they will no longer trust us for anything.

FIX THE BAD HABIT –
NON-JUDGMENTAL PLANNING

Take that volunteering and use it to assist in proving them wrong. What do you like to do that you could share? Do you like to sing, dance, play an instrument, have a pet, do you have some kind of art? Any of these or any other talent could be shared with anyone. Take for example you play an instrument. Volunteer to play that instrument at nursing homes, foster care, and hospitals. Not only will you get to share something yo enjoy, but you will show others your talent, give them something to look forward to, and stimulate them to enjoy music.

Judgments of what is wrong can lead to making good judgments. Take it as constructive criticism and hear it out before replying. It may not be right, but even a little is progress.   Show your positive judgment and give compliments when due. It will help others sense how happy, kind, courteous, and emotionally stable you are and treat you with dignity.

Judgmental people tend to be jealous or have low self-esteem. They like to bring you down to make you feel at the same level. Remember you don't need them in your life so do what makes you happy and don't worry about them, you can remove them from your life so what they think doesn't matter. Do what you want to do, do not worry about them.

12. COOKING- GOOD HABITS

Keep the areas clean and utensils safe. Keep the floors and counters clean and disinfected, the cutting boards non-slip, knives sharp, and clean up as you go when cooking. Throw away the scraps and wipe up the spills as you go. Any spices, seasoning, should near the stove, and wine, vinegar, and oils should be kept near the stove, but on a top shelf out of the reach of children.

Any leftovers should be saved so that they can be used as a side dish or as an ingredient in another dinner. For example, homemade macaroni and cheese can be the main course one night, and then what is left of it can be used as a side dish the next night with meat. If they are made in reverse order and there is meat leftover, cut it into small pieces and put it into the macaroni and cheese before baking. There is also the option of freezing any leftovers or using them for lunch the next day.

COOKING – BAD HABITS

Some cooking and baking habits are not safe but are not even known to be dangerous. Don't preheat the cooking surface, it only makes the cooking time different and can cause food burns and uneven cooking. When it comes to measuring flour, don't dip it in the flour bag and level it off, dip it lightly or sift it into the cup, and then level it off at the top. Overfilling and stirring too often when cooking removes the steam and heat, so it takes longer to cook, and sometimes it can cause undercooking. Meat needs to be rinsed before cooked and set to rest before a cut. Pyrex pans are not good for broiler recipes, they can shatter if they get too hot.

FIX THE BAD HABIT – COOKING PLANNING

Food needs to be cooked thoroughly to be safe to consume. However, if you are trying to rush there are things that you are doing that can cause food to not be thoroughly cooked. Plan dinners ahead of time so that you do not have to rush. Being able to go at a slower pace will allow you to have the flame at the suggested or low level, adjust how ingredients are handled so they are correct, and wash the pots and pans as needed so the correct ones are used. Keep the cooking area clean. Keeping up with it as you go helps you keep the food area clean and safe.

13. EATING – GOOD HABITS

Planning meals at home ahead of time not only saves you the time and thought when you get hungry, but it gives you the chance to make it well balanced. Some foods are easier to digest and some that can stimulate the metabolism to increase. Eat slowly and enjoy that food. When it comes to time for a dessert, people naturally think of something sweet like cake, pie, cookies, etc., but how about a sweet fruit or yogurt? Both are healthy and can be sweet if it's the right kind. Put the food that you know you need to use to cook with, in locations near the stove and food that is for the kids in locations they can reach. For the ingredients like wine, vinegar, and others that are useful, but not kid-safe, put them in inconvenient locations like a top shop or the basement.

EATING – BAD HABITS

Eating is supposed to be to give the body nutrients, but many times people use it as an escape or distraction. Some of the most common bad eating habits are eating when tired and stressed. Other habits will cause weight gain such as binge eating, eating too fast, feeling like you have to eat everything on your plate, eating when you're not hungry, desserts, skipping breakfast, or just eating unhealthy food regularly. Boredom can cause you to look in the cupboard for something. At that time it doesn't matter to you if it is healthy or junk food. You are not hungry, just looking for quick, easy eating like drive-through windows, vending machines, and microwaveable food.

FIX THE BAD HABIT – EATING PLANNING

The best way to change an eating habit is to sit down and write out what type of eating habits you currently have and want to change. There can be circumstances that stimulate you to eat, figure out what the stimulants. A common one is television time, so have healthy snacks around for that time. When getting groceries, have a list of the healthy meals to make, healthy and easy to grab and eat snacks, and do NOT make these lists when you are hungry. You know what you can and cannot eat and you know when you tend to eat the most and worst kinds of food. Find something like BBQ pork rinds to leave on the coffee table in the living room to provoke its consumption instead of that bag of Doritos in the kitchen on the top shelf.

14. ALCOHOL GOOD HABITS

When people think of alcohol habits they think of the dangers, but it does have benefits too. It has been found that red wine can slightly improve cardiovascular health by reducing coronary artery disease. HDL (High-Density Lipoproteins) or good cholesterol that lessens the chances of blood clots is also helped by red wine consumption. This can reduce the risk of heart attack or stroke and it contains resveratrol. Resveratrol is a compound that contains antioxidant properties that help fight pathogens that occur in the body. Beer is also known to assist with cholesterol by decreasing HDL cholesterol over time. 38% of beer drinkers are less likely to have osteoporosis and 20% had a lower risk of hip fractures because of the silicon in beer.

ALCOHOL BAD HABITS

Alcohol can trigger some medical issues such as chronic asthma and migraines. There have been links to certain cancers to excessive alcohol intakes such as hepatocellular cancer, liver cancer, esophageal cancer, and gastrointestinal cancer. This is because alcohol can damage cells in the body that are hard for the body to repair. If there is a history of diabetes, alcohol affects blood sugar levels and impacts diabetes medication. This can cause hypoglycemia, aka insulin shock and then there is the infamous heart failure that excessive drinking weakens the heart muscles that slows down the pumping of blood properly leading to cardiovascular conditions and congestive heart failure. There is also the fact that some people cannot drink without consuming too much and the results cause them not to think clearly and some become abusive or drink and drive.

FIX THE BAD HABIT – ALCOHOL PLANNING

If alcohol is consumed in moderation it can be healthy and beneficial to the body. There are long term medical conditions that are decreased if alcohol consumption is regulated and not excessive. The effects of alcohol consumption are different for men and women. It is considered safe for women to have one drink a day and it is considered safe for men to have two per day when they are within what is considered the normal weight. These quantities change if the individual has any health issues or obtains any as they age. If there is a form of a medical condition such as migraines, asthma, cancers, or dangerous living conditions because of alcohol such as unclear living choices that affect both families and driving choices there is help available. See some of the extra help that is listed at the end of the references. Use it for health benefits, entertainment, enjoyment, and relaxation.

15. GAMBLING GOOD HABITS

Gambling is misinterpreted by people. It is taking chances in the circumstances when not in full control of the outcome. People that are starting a new business are gambling, people that are trying a new haircut are gambling, people that are going back to college are gambling. It is moving out of the normal realm. So, take for example a time when there is a bad situation at work and you are in the middle of it. You have options, of giving information to the correct people, looking for a new job, or just keeping quiet. You may be taking chances to get out of the realm or ride the waves and wait for the outcome. So do you step out of the safety zone and take chances? Life is full of chances to make a difference, if it is not what you want, do some research, and take a gamble. Live your life to the fullest, sometimes you may not get the total results, but you may just get out of the bad situation and move on. You will still be happier.

Actual gambling with finance can also be healthy entertainment. The research found that gamblers have less alcohol and substance abuse, less depression, and less mental health treatment, and have better general health. They are not incarcerated and filing bankruptcy as much as those that do not gamble. Healthy people like to gamble and they tend to be happier from the satisfaction than those that sit and watch television. Gambling is a learning experience with a complex strategy that can be mastered. It instigates the mind to do the math, read facial and body expressions while working on restraining one's expressions. It is a way to relax and get away from everyday stress such as home and work while socializing. In the end, it instigates money management for the now and future game situations, that can be used in future life situations.

GAMBLING- BAD HABITS

The American Psychiatric Association (APA) has included gambling in the fifth edition of the Diagnostic and Statistical Manual because it can be an addiction. There are entertainment and problem gambling. Problem gambling is harmful to health both psychologically and physically. It can cause depression, migraines, distress, intestinal disorders, and many other problems that are related to anxiety. It has been known to lead people to feel lonely, despondent, and even suicidal. It is an emotional problem that has financial results and the disorder affects not only family and friends, but employment. People that are addicted to gambling feel the need to increase money by gambling and are restless when they do not get to gamble. They will attempt to stop, but feel distressed and return to feel complete. They will lie to family and friends to keep it a secret and lose their and others' money, which causes relationship problems. There are common triggers to develop a gambling addiction, but the most common are retirement, traumatic circumstance, employment and family stress, loneliness, and anxiety.

FIX THE BAD HABIT –
GAMBLING PLANNING

Gambling can be fun entertainment with friends. It can be the perfect night out to just get away from the daily stress and be harmless fun. It can be the opportunity to look at a situation and justify taking a chance that would normally not occur to you or give you the will to make a bigger move. However, it can b addictive and have negative effects psychologically, physically, and socially.   It becomes a problem when person cannot stop doing it and it causes negative effects on any area of their life. There are different types of treatment available for those addicted to gambling such as Therapy, medication, and self-help groups. Don't always think of gambling as related to money. There are many times in life when we are making decisions that are also gambling, we just don't realize it. Take life gambling as an opportunity, not a risk.

16. EXERCISING GOOD HABITS

After any kind of surgery check with a doctor or therapist before starting exercise. It can be a healthy regime but needs to be done when your body allows. It is one of the best ways to stop the pain, especially in the back. The two most important things to do are warm-up and cool down before and after exercising. Always support your spine and strengthen your muscles that support your spine like doing a pelvic tilt, knee-to-chest, or hamstring stretch. Water exercises are great for back muscles. Water aerobics and swimming increase strength in the back and even walking in the water is good for backaches. Sign up for a Yoga class that is especially for back strengthening. The instructor will know the limitations and can adapt for back pain, they will instruct on the Swiss ball for stretching and strengthening. Another way to increase the back strength is to take the stairs, but use the railing, keep the back straight the entire time, and when you put a foot down on a step, place the foot flat so the entire foot is on the step, not just the toe.

EXERCISING BAD HABITS

If you have had back surgery, there are common exercises that are not healthy for you to do until you get approval from your doctor. The worst exercise to do is a full sit-up, and the second-worst is leg lifts down while on the floor lying on your back. Keeping legs straight and bending over to try and touch toes is not a good exercise after back surgery along with one that requires weights in hands with twists and bends. It is not good to do anything kind of jogging, running, or high-impact aerobics. Anything that takes place on a hard surface like tennis and dance can jar or twist the spine. Some bad habits are going to the gym without authorization from a doctor or therapist, not having a spotter, and not having a coach suggested routine.

FIX THE BAD HABIT –
EXERCISING ENHANCING

When it comes to your health do not assume that you can or cannot do something based on pain. See a doctor or therapist and get recommendations first. Restricting yourself due to pain or over-exerting yourself because you feel fine can cause it to get worse. Take the time to make a phone call, telecommunicate, or send an email before making a change in your daily routine after corrective surgery. It's great to do for yourself, but when you get the okay to exercise, have a spotter and a routine that has been recommended by a coach.

17. CLEANING GOOD HABITS

Start the day by making the bed as soon as you get out of it. It is quick and an accomplishment to make you feel good. As you see things that are arrays, pick them up and put them where they belong or throw them out, then wipe down the area. That can keep the area from clutter and prevent grime. Set up an area for all the daily papers like schoolwork, newspapers, bills, etc. This keeps paper from getting mixed up and lost. Clean out the refrigerator weekly on garbage day. This will keep the refrigerator from smelling, anything that is expired will be removed promptly, and write what needs to be replaced on the grocery list. Do a load of laundry each day. Throw it in the washer in the morning, in the dryer when making dinner, and fold and put away just before you sit down for the night. This will keep the number of dirty clothes regulated and not make it an all-day activity. If you have a dishwasher, put the dishes in right after dinner and once it is full, run it and put them away before you sit down for the night. If you do them by hand, wash the right up and leave them in the strainer to be put away before you sit down for the night.

When it comes to an actual house cleaning, set a schedule of what to clean when. It can be a schedule such as one chore a day, dust Monday, vacuum Tuesday, sweep Wednesday, mop Thursday, etc. to do after dinner or just pick a day of the week and set aside the necessary time to do all of it, but don't forget to treat yourself, when you're done!.

CLEANING- BAD HABITS

Many commercial products that are advertised are damaging to the environment and our health. They are not any more effective at cleaning. Using too much of a cleaning product is not cleaning it better, but leaving a layer that needs to be removed. So waxing that floor with too much wax for shine, makes a wax buildup, and less shine. There is, of course, the neglect of reading directions, which again can cause an overdose. It has also been found that bleach isn't as effective as it was once thought to be.

The sponge and not closing the wet shower curtain can cause cross-contamination, mold, and mildew to develop which defeats cleaning. Finding excuses not to clean will only make it more difficult and time-consuming. This can be seen when it comes to doing dishes and hoarding what is thought to be necessary including the cleaning supplies and trying to find them later. Don't make it more work than it already is.

FIX THE BAD HABIT –
CLEANING PLANNING

The frustration of finding the time to clean can be enough to make cleaning unbearable, let alone when th necessary items are difficult to find. How about when the work is done and it looks worse because the cleaning was not done properly. Take the time to read the directions on the cleaning agent and follow it. In the closet clean out the unused, unnecessary supplies, and throw them away when they are expired. With the busy schedules in today's world it can be difficult to find time to clean, let alone the ambition to clean; so se a schedule. When it is completed, treat yourself to wha you want. Not only will you get to give yourself something, but you will also feel relieved to know that if anyone drops by, you are ready for them!

18. AFTER WORK – GOOD HABITS

It is hard to believe that the activities that you do and don't do after work can have such an effect on your happiness. Some of this may sound like repeats, but that just shows that what is good for you then is also good for you after work to get out of the rut. Take time for yourself to rejuvenate, sit in silence for 10 minutes, and listen to yourself take deep breaths while you relax your body or burn off the stress with an exercise. Let those mood-stabilizing endorphins go and calm those nerves. Spend time with nature and friends; both are great ways to take your mind away from what stresses it. Escape from reality in a book and allow yourself to go to sleep earlier. Plan what needs to be done the next day and how it can be done in the most productive time-consuming way to give you time to take your pet for a walk, meditate. Eat healthily and exercise regularly to keep a balance in your mind and body.

AFTER WORK – BAD HABITS

Sad but true, there are more after work bad habits than there are good habits. These bad habits can hinder your productivity if they are not managed, it can be like going from work to work. It makes you want to go home and melt into Netflix with a TV dinner and watch an entire season or just go out for a happy hour and stay out too long. Trying to multitask to get too many things done at the same time can backfire and make more work to fix what went wrong. Concentration needs to be done for certain tasks or cause more problems. An example of this is when a new school year starts and you don't have the kids on a routine in the morning to get around for the bus, their homework isn't started before dinner. Or you not having dinner ideas before you leave for work so you don't pull meat from the freezer can cause additional stress trying to think of something quick and easy at the last minute. Being a night owl or stress can cause you to stay up too late and then not getting enough sleep can cause more stress. Junk food or an unhealthy dinner can cause your body to react and keep you awake. It's a repetitive circle.

FIX THE BAD HABIT –
AFTER WORK PLANNING

There needs to be a "social recovery" time between the two worlds of work and home to decompress. It can be a chat on the elevator or a friendly text with a friend, but the transition without "work" is essential. Look at some of the things you do weekdays after work and think about which ones are productive and which ones are causing more work or stress. Having a regime to do what needs to be done can be set so you have time to do for you after work. You can set it up to do more than one activity at a time with the right people or in the right location to make it more fun than you ever imagined. This is for you, take your dog for a walk, go to the beach, throw a frisbee with a friend, go out to dinner with family. It's your life, do it for you.

19. LEISURE TIME – GOOD HABITS

What is done during the time of leisure can impact an attitude, career, family, health, and more. Exercise for 30 minutes a day, 5 days a week can help the mood, brain health, and increase productivity. If there are hobbies that you enjoy, do them when you have leisure time. You can have some fun and open your mind to your creativeness or learning more from it through experience and research. Mindfulness is a way to give the brain a break. Forget the world and everything in it with all your senses relaxed for 10 minutes.

Some less fortunate people could use your time, skills, and your family's skills to build their self-esteem. Use your leisure time to do for the less fortunate. You get the fulfillment of sharing, success, and appreciation while sharing the time of helping others with your own family.

LEISURE TIME – BAD HABITS

Reading social media can seem like a good leisure time activity to get your mind off of things, but many times it does just the opposite. It has multiple subject matters displayed that will get you thinking, not relaxing. Eating junk food tends to be done when boredom arises, but this can cause sleepiness and weight gain. There are all kinds of shopping available on the internet and TV that may seem easier, but the added unexpected expense can cause problems in the future. It is easy to buy what you don't need because it looks good and you don't want to miss it, but don't short the utility bill for it.

FIX THE BAD HABIT –
LEISURE TIME PLANNING

Going onto multimedia for entertainment can be fun but it can also be stressful and it makes it easy to sit with chips and soda while reading it. The advertisements that are seen between posts might strike you to do shopping that you don't need to do and spend money that you do not want to spend. Skipping getting daily exercise can come from the distractions of email, multimedia, and the news. Put the smartphone away, close that laptop, and shut off that TV. This will allow you to look at what you want to accomplish during this opportunity to enjoy making yourself, family, friends, and the less fortunate to feel better without distractions

20. DRUGS – GOOD HABITS

When people hear the word drugs they automatically think negatively, but that is not necessarily always the case. There are OTC (Over the Counter) drugs that are not negative and some have positive and productive usage. Take into consideration common medication like vitamins, minerals that are FDA (Food and Drug Administration) approved. To be FDA approved it cannot contain contaminants or impurities and they are labeled with the Good Manufacturing Practice Standards. Some examples of good vitamins and minerals are Vitamin C approved for scurvy, Melatonin approved for insomnia or sleeping assistance, Magnesium approved for muscle and nerve function and regulating blood pressure, Echinacea boosting immunity, and Potassium to help muscles like control heartbeat and breathing. The next time your body is not feeling right think about if you have changed your diet and you might be shorting yourself a vitamin.

DRUGS –
BAD HABITS

Drugs that make people feel good, stop feeling bad, and peer pressure are the most common reasons for drug usage. Depression, anxiety, and inadequacy can cause people the feel more able to be like others. At first, the drug may be prescribed for the pain, but there can be a "high" feeling that comes as a side effect. Sometimes the "high" or escape is overly enjoyed and then enhanced by taking too many or in the wrong manner, which can cause an addiction. Different drugs have different impacts on your brain and body.

There are also common habit drugs like Marijuana, Opioids, Heroin, Cocaine, LSD, and Inhalants. These drugs affect parts of the body and the mind like heart rate changes. They can cause heart attacks, breathing, seizures, paranoia, trouble sleeping, coma, brain damage, and even death. All of these drugs are hard to control the urge, and some are harder to stop even though it is known that it is causing physical, mental, and social harm.

FIX THE BAD HABIT –
DRUG USAGE PLANNING

Keep your body regulated naturally by taking vitamins and minerals that your body may feel a shortage of due to exercise and diet changes. If it is a prescription follow the medical professional's usage suggestions. If it is illegal, don't start the drug and get help now. The longer the usage of drugs before the decision to stop, the more addicted, and the harder it is to stop. This is from changes in how the brain works because of the drugs. They can cause harmful behaviors that can get worse and get harder to control. The best is to not try it or stick to the regimen prescribed by the doctor. If you start to find interest in getting more of the drug, get help right away to make it easier for you and everyone in your life.

21. TRAVELING – GOOD HABITS

Traveling is supposed to be a fun getaway or a business-related. Here are some tips to make it easier to get started. Anything that is a value such as ID's, medication, and passports should be put in the luggage that is carry-on or kept close by. Bring along empty water bottles. If you are at a terminal, once past security you can fill it at a water fountain or just have one in your vehicle to keep hydrated. The air where you are going can be so different from what you are accustomed to. Take pictures of all of your identification, credit cards, ATM, etc. and send them to your google drive account or someone you can trust that will be able to retrieve them for you in case they are lost or stolen.

TRAVELING – BAD HABITS

It is hard to believe that even while on a vacation away from everyday routines, research shows that people still spend time on their social networks and cell phones. Being on these cell phones also causes an obsession with taking pictures that are not even relevant to the trip. If you are traveling where there is a different language, don't expect them to know what you are saying. Waiting too long to pack is common and then the items that you wanted or that are necessary are forgotten. It may even cause the trip to be more expensive because there are fewer options and the costs increase.

FIX THE BAD HABIT –
TRAVEL PLANNING

Travel whether it is for work or fun is to leave the usual life behind. Leave the media and cell phones at the hotel. They are not going anywhere and the necessary people know you are traveling and they should leave you alone. If you are going to another country, learn the simple basic words before your trip, and there are applications available to assist with translation. Don't expect them to know the language of all visitors. Write out an itinerary of where you would like to visit from highest to lowest interest and by location. Don't spend too much time looking at the map or through the brochures for directions. If you don't find it move on to the next place on the list. Having a list of items to pack in your suitcase zipper makes the chances of forgetting things less likely along with the chances of bringing too much. You also won't forget the mandatory or significant things for your handbag or carry on.

22. SELF- DETERMINATION – GOOD HABITS

Having confidence in oneself can help a person in multiple different ways including choices in their life. They have a more successful behavior, are more determined. From this, they have positive outcomes even after experiencing many failures. They desire to grow, master a challenge or are just looking forward to experiences that make them develop a complete sense of self. Their reliability tends to be very high along with their rates of accomplishment.

SELF – DETERMINATION – BAD HABITS

When there is something that needs to be done or we think we want to do but know that there will be a lot of work, we tend to do things to keep ourselves from progressing. We use an alibi from others; we even set up things to happen for an excuse. We will wait for the right moment to start or even wait for a sign or an okay from someone else before proceeding. We want things to be easy, so we wait for the perfect time or setting and if we don't get it, we use that as an excuse to not pursue it. Results are going to happen, sometimes good, sometimes bad, but don't worry about them. What happens to you is your business, not anyone else's, so don't compare yourself to them.

FIX THE BAD HABIT –
SELF DETERMINATION ENHANCING

Think about what you do and how you do it. If it is not right, assess it and try something different next time, but at least keep trying. Don't take everything too seriously and don't spend too much time doing the things you don't like, think of another way to do it or you will lose what little drive you have. To feel complete to yourself, behavior and communication skills need to have techniques that satisfy the needs of your goal. There needs to be a focus set by you that is within reach to feel progress. Making the use of skills such as choice, determination, problem-solving, goal setting and attainment, self-regulation, self-advocacy, efficiency, and awareness will help in the skills development for determination in self-improvement. Reward yourself continuously.

23. HANDLING ISSUES GOOD HABITS

Things happen unexpectedly at different times in our lives. Put a small amount of money aside every paycheck and leave it for an emergency fund or in case of a financial crisis. Always be willing to face reality and start working to improve right from the moment an issue is noticed. Present solutions that you are unsure of to an outside source. They often see things differently or can point out things you missed. Breaking down the issue to find the source or assigning parts of it to individuals can relieve a lot of the tension the issue is causing and different perspectives. Remember what has worked and modify what didn't.

HANDLING ISSUES – BAD HABITS

Some of the most common issues are faced by everyone, but the issues are never the same and how they are handled makes a difference. Some people like to blame others for their problems. Then they feel that those who created the problems are responsible to fix it too. It doesn't work that way. Even if something someone else did cause a problem for you, it's up to you to do something to fix it. When someone came into work sick and you caught the illness, they are not going to buy the medicine for you that worked for them. There are reactions or routines that you may need to change over time to keep up with the changes around you. These changes can adjust your perspective.

FIX THE BAD HABIT-
HANDLING ISSUES PLANNING

Check to see what your attitude is presenting. If you are feeling disadvantaged, overlooked it could be because of the communication that you are presenting. Look around and see what is different between you and those that are succeeding and are successful. Don't let life feel like a burden, get out, and enjoy it. When an issue arises, start working on it as soon as possible to make progress by communicating and getting information now instead of later. Don't just blame them and leave it or use it as an excuse. It's only going to get fixed or better if you do something about it, nobody else cares how it is affecting you. If you fix the issue, you will have success and it will be noted by you and others. Collect as much information as you can to fix it and show them that they have nothing on you!

24. OPTIMISTIC DISPOSITION – GOOD HABIT

Optimistic people believe that good things will happen to them. Research shows those that are optimistic experience adversity when working towards a goal. They will reassess the steps they have used or research for different approaches and this expands their chances of achievement. They tend to be more persistent in obtaining goals and they use direct actions with a plan. This helps them to be open-minded to cope with problems.

PESSIMISTIC DISPOSITION – BAD HABIT

Pessimistic people believe that bad things will happen to them. Pessimists tend to look at adversity as a sign that it is not meant to be, is not going to work, or just give up. "If it was meant to be it will be" or "it's out of my hands" tends to be their perception. They do not have a high rate of enthusiasm to try things. Cognitive styles like depression and pessimism can affect experience thoughts. An example of this would be even in a positive result situation, still seeing what it is missing, what else could have happened, or comparing to others that had better results.

FIX THE BAD HABIT –
OPTIMISTIC DISPOSITION ENHANCING

Goals are what we base our lives around. Whether it is a career goal, family goal, or just a simple what's for dinner goal. All of these goals give meaning to our lives and future. Although optimism and pessimism are personality traits, they are based on the expectancy of human goal experience. Problem-focused strategies with active attempts and optimism lead to some advancement and learning. However, pessimism strategies lead to what is perceived as wasted effort. Research shows that those that are optimistic generally have higher achievements and better physical and mental well-being. If you have the habit of seeing the glass as half empty not half full, try to perceive things a little differently. The half-empty glass is bigger and better. It also means that you are looking at the good side of the situation.

Here are some miscellaneous bad habits and suggestions to stop them or just good habits suggestions to make life easier:

25. BRAGGING – DOMINANCE IN CONVERSATIONS

Conversations are for communication or discussion. When people feel they know the most of the subject they tend to take over the conversation and become domineering. They can be unconscious of their character and sometimes go into a bragging spree, which bores the audience and they block out any other person talking. This is also common when there is a discussion or argument and a person thinks they are right. They tend to block out what the other person is saying because they are thinking of what they are going to say in a reply. When one of the arguing parties does this, there is less likely a chance of a resolution because they do not actually hear what the other is saying so an agreement cannot be made.

This makes for unfair communication, misguided information and does not allow for any negotiations many times. All of these forms of conversation lead to non-resolution or non-benefit because there isn't an agreement in a one-sided conversation.

FIX THE BAD HABIT-
STOPPING BRAGGING PLANNING

Confrontation and changing the subject is a way to let them know that you do not admire them. Looking away from them or appearing bored may make them feel awkward around you. You can then say something impressive about yourself to show them that you have it too, but then say something polite to make it known that you are not bragging like "sorry, I realize that is not your area." You could also tell about someone else who is better in what they are bragging about, but stay overly polite and walk away. They will either understand or be perplexed; either way, they won't feel the dominance power anymore.

If you are a bragger, stop and think about other people and their feelings. How will they react to what you are saying to them? Are you being selfish and not listening to them? Are you letting say anything? Are you thinking about what they are saying?

Being a bragger makes you appear to be a selfish, self-centered person that people do not want to be around. So unless you want to be alone and only talk to yourself; stop being so rude and take other people into consideration as a result of what you say and do.

DEEP BREATHING –
GOOD HABIT PLANNING

Most people do not realize how beneficial extra oxygen is to the body and the mind. It cleans, soothes, opens, and is part of our being. Deep breathing decreases stress and stimulates calmness. Cortisol is a stress hormone that your brain releases under pressure. Taking deep breaths puts more oxygen into your body and your heart relaxes. This informs your brain to rela: and release those endorphins that make you feel good and these endorphins also help with the pain. When carbon monoxide is fully released from the body in breathing 70 % of the toxins are removed, the other 30% is removed by the bladder and bowels. The stamina of your body will increase with the higher oxygen in the blood and this will also increase immunity because of nutrients, and vitamin efficiency increases. Blood vessel dilation will occur as muscles relax and this will decrease blood pressure and improve digestion.

Not only does deep breathing release stress, but it also assists with anxiety, pain, high blood pressure, immunity, and even digestion. The cleaner the blood, the healthier the body, and the better you feel. Proper deep breathing is slow and gentle and deep enough to feel the stomach expand.

A simple way to do this that can be done just about anywhere is to concentrate on inhaling through the nose and exhaling through the mouth while in a comfortable chair, but be careful….you might put yourself to sleep. Try to work deep breathing into your daily routine or at least three times a week. It will lower the amount of stress you feel and help you think more clearly.

ASSUMING – BAD HABIT

We don't even realize that we assume. It can start as easily as childhood and assuming there will be three meals a day every day. Then we start to do it when we receiving half the information and filling in the blanks from what we have known in circumstances from the past instead of asking. The blanks are filled in by what is perceived or remembered. However, the circumstances may be different. The perception may not be from the right location or without significant information.

When emotions are involved it gets even worse because we tend to remember the painful first and react. This causes less willingness to step up and express oneself, go on auto defense, and pick a fight or just create negative feelings on those around you.

FIX THE BAD HABIT-
STOPPING ASSUMING PLANNING

One of the best examples of how wrong assuming can be is when driving. You cannot assume you know where every driver you encounter is going, how they are going to get there, and what they are doing or thinking at that moment.

Assuming can become toxic to not only to you but to everyone in your life. The next time you start to feel that deep pain, nauseous feeling like in your stomach, or your adrenaline increases from an assumption, remember that you are doing it to yourself. Your resistance stops your growth, your stunted growth stops you from moving forward, and you start to blame others.

Stop the habit of jumping to conclusions from the past that may not even be relevant. People change age and ways of life. It may have been that it was painful, toxic, and wrong, but don't assume it is that again. Just ask! The results are going to be a surprise to you.

REFERENCES:

10 Bad Cleaning Habits You Need to Break! Electrodry Carpet Cleaning, Copyright 2019. Retrieved on October 17, 2020, from https://www.electrodry.com.au/news-blog/10-bad-cleaning-habits-you-need-to-break/

10 Bad Cooking Habits You Should Break, September 25, 2018, from EatingWell. Retrieved on October 6, 2020, from http://www.eatingwell.com/article/69202/10-bad-cooking-habits-you-should-break/

10 Bad Habits you need to bread to be More Productive, Productivity, Time Management. Retrieved on October 17, 2020, from https://bestlifeonline.com/after-work-habits-productivity/?nab=1

10 Thinking Habits for Unlimited Personal Growth, from Calling. Copyright 2020. Retrieved on October 17, 2020, from https://bestlifeonline.com/after-work-habits-productivity/?nab=1

10 Unhealthy Habits You Need to Break, by Brierley Horton. Published by EatingWell on February 19, 2012. Retrieved on October 5, 2020, from http://www.eatingwell.com/article/275602/10-unhealthy-habits-you-need-to-break-now/

12 Bad Health Habits and How To Fix Them, by Amberly McAteer. Published in Prevention & Recovery. Retrieved on October 7, 2020, from https://www.canadianliving.com/health/prevention-and-

recovery/article/12-bad-health-habits-and-how-to-fix-them

13 Common Bad Habits that Hold You Back from Success, by Mario Christou. Published on Lifehack. Retrieved on October 17, 2020, from https://www.lifehack.org/articles/productivity/13-common-bad-habits-that-hold-you-back-from-success.html

13 Common Life Problems and How to Fix Them, By Leon Ho. Published July 2, 2020, on Lifehack. Retrieved on October 18, 2020, from https://www.lifehack.org/articles/lifehack/7-steps-to-resolve-any-problem.html

17 After-Work Habits Killing Your Productivity, Don't Let Your Evening Routine Sabotage Your Nine-To-Five, By Desiree O. Published, January 2, 2019. Retrieved on October 17, 2020, from https://bestlifeonline.com/after-work-habits-productivity/?nab=1

18 Reasons Why a Daily Routine Is So important. Published by Skilled at Life. Retrieved on October 20, 2020, from http://www.skilledatlife.com/18-reasons-why-a-daily-routine-is-so-important/

19 Healthy Family Habits to Try. Published by Ask the Scientists. Retrieved on October 23, from https://askthescientists.com/healthy-family-habits/

20 Good Habits that Can Help You Stay Healthy. Published on Brunet (Copyright 2020). Retrieved on October 21,

from https://www.brunet.ca/en/health/health-tips/20-good-habits-that-can-help-you-stay-healthy/

21 Self-Determination Skills and Activities to Utilize Today, by Elaine Houston, BSc. Published on PositivePsychology.com October 13, 2020. Retrieved on October 17, 2020, from https://positivepsychology.com/self-determination-skills-activities/

24 Bad Travel Habits You should Avoid, Khol Nguyen, from the Broad Life, published on November 15, 2019, Retrieved on October 17, 2020, from https://thebroadlife.com/24-bad-travel-habits.html

4 Hobbies That Will Lead to Excellent Habits, by Alana Harvey. Published on Lifehack. Retrieved on October 15, 2020, from https://www.lifehack.org/496700/4-hobbies-that-will-lead-to-excellent-habits

5 Gen X Bad Habits our Children Should Not Adopt, by Matt Boresi. Published on Chicago Parent, June 6, 2016. Retrieved on October 9, 2020, from https://www.chicagoparent.com/learn/general-parenting/gen-x/

5 Ways to Deal With Someone Who Never Stops Bragging, When enough is enough, Psychology Today. Posted October 15, 2016, By Andrea F. Polard, Psy.D. Copyright 2016 from https://www.psychologytoday.com/us/blog/unified-theory-happiness/201610/5-ways-deal-someone-who-never-stops-bragging

7 Elements of Successful Goal Achievements, by Mark
Pettit, Strategic Business Coach. (Copyright 2020)
Published on May 12, 2020. Retrieved on October 23,
2020, from https://thriveglobal.com/stories/7-key-
elements-of-successful-goal-achievement/

7 Healthy Habits for Greater Physical & Mental Well-Being.
(Copyright 2020) Published September 20, 2017, in H-
Wave. Retrieved on October 8, 2020, from
https://www.h-wave.com/blog/7-healthy-habits-for-
greater-physical-and-mental-well-being/

8 Powerful Mental Health Habits from a Professional
Psychologist. Published April 26, 2018, in
NickWIgnall. Retrieved on October 4, 2020, from
https://nickwignall.com/mental-health-habits/

8 Small Cooking Habits That Make a Big Difference,
February 20, 2013, from Kitchn. Retrieved on October
6, 2020, from https://www.thekitchn.com/8-small-
cooking-habits-that-make-a-big-difference-184414

9 Habits of People Who Always Have a Clean House, By
Southern Living Editors, Published on February 17,
2017, Copyright 2020. Retrieved on October 17, 2020,
from
https://www.southernliving.com/home/organization/cle
an-house-habits

9 Reasons Why Judging People is a Very Bad Habit by
Divyani Rattanpal, Updated July 16, 2014. Published
in Shutterstock (Copyright 2020), Retrieved on October
21, 2020, from https://www.mensxp.com/special-

features/today/23352-9-reasons-why-judging-people-is-a-very-bad-habit.html

9 Things that Stop You From Achieving Your Goals, by Lidiya K. Published on March 5, 2015, by Success Advice. Retrieved on October 16, 2020, from https://addicted2success.com/success-advice/9-things-that-stop-you-from-achieving-your-goals/

A Vitamin Approved as a Drug (!): Forget what you think you know to be True from Camargo Pharmaceutical Services. Copyright 2020. Retrieved on October 17, 2020, from https://bestlifeonline.com/after-work-habits-productivity/?nab=1

Alcohol, Drug, Gambling Help

Benefits of Deep Breathing, by UB Therapist Andrea Watkins LCSW. Published on Urban Balance Copyright 2019. Retrieved on October 18, 2020, from https://urbanbalance.com/benefits-deep-breathing/

Benefits, uses, and side effects of Echinacea. Published in Medical News Today. Copyright 2004-2020. Retrieved on October 17, 2020, from https://www.medicalnewstoday.com/articles/252684

Centers for Disease Control and Prevention, Alcohol, and Public Health. U.S Department of Health & Human Services, USA. Gov. Updated September 3, 2020. Retrieved on October 10, 2020, https://www.cdc.gov/alcohol/index.htm

How Healthy After-Work Habits Can Boost Happiness, by Isadora Baum, CHC. Published on October 11, 2016.

Retrieved on October 17, 2020, from
https://www.electrodry.com.au/news-blog/10-bad-
cleaning-habits-you-need-to-break/

How to Deal with Peer Pressure as an Adult. Sylvia
Brafman Mental Health Center. Retrieved from:
http://www.mentalhealthcenter.org/how-to-deal-with-
peer-pressure-as-an-adult/

How Your Bad Habits Affect Your Health, WebMD
(Copyright 2005-2020). Retrieved on October 1, 2020:
https://www.webmd.com/balance/ss/slideshow-bad-
habits

Improving Your Eating Habits, Healthy Weight, Nutrition,
and Physical Activity, Centers for Disease Control and
Prevention. U.S Department of Health & Human
Services, USA. Gov. Updated August 17, 2020.
Retrieved on October 10, 2020, from
https://www.cdc.gov/healthyweight/losing_weight/eatin
g_habits.html

Letters to the Editors, When hobbies become obsessions:
why too much of a good thing can be a bad thing.
Published by Discover. Retrieved on October 15 from
https://amp.scmp.com/yp/discover/your-voice/letters-
editorial/article/3066381/when-hobbies-become-
obsessions-why-too

Melatonin, Vitamins & Supplements. Published in Web
MD. Copyright 2005-2020. Retrieved on October 17,
2020, from https://bestlifeonline.com/after-work-habits-
productivity/?nab=1

National Council on Problem Gambling, (Copyright 2014), Retrieved on October 11, 2020, from https://www.ncpgambling.org/help-treatment/national-helpline-1-800-522-4700/

National Institute on Alcohol Abuse and Alcoholism. Retrieved on October 10, 2020, from https://www.niaaa.nih.gov/

News Flash: Too Much Planning is Just as Bad as Procrastination, by Lilly Herman. Published in the Daily Muse. Copyright 2020. Retrieved on October 22, 2020, from https://www.google.com/amp/s/www.themuse.com/amp/advice/news-flash-too-much-planning-is-just-as-bad-as-procrastination

Optimism and Pessimism. Published on Psychology. Retrieved on October 18, 2020, from http://psychology.iresearchnet.com/counseling-psychology/personality-traits/optimism-and-pessimism-counseling/

Peer Pressure and Teenagers, from Reachout.com. (Copyright 2020) Retrieved on October 14, 2020, from https://parents.au.reachout.com/common-concerns/everyday-issues/peer-pressure-and-teenagers

Planning Ahead: 4 Reasons Why it Keeps You Sane, by Dr. Carol Morgan. Published in the HuffPost on May 4, 2017. Retrieved on October 22, 2020, from https://m.huffpost.com/us/entry/us_9823950

Rush, Health & Wellness, to Drink, or Not to Drink? The
     health benefits - and risks - of alcohol. Copyright of
     Rush University Medical Center. Retrieved on October
     10, 2020, from https://www.rush.edu/health-
     wellness/discover-health/alcohol-good-or-bad-you

Signs Your Daily Routine is Killing Your Productivity, by
     Kat Boogaard. Published by the Muse, July 6, 2016.
     Retrieved on October 22, 2020, from
     https://www.inc.com/the-muse/5-signs-daily-routine-
     killing-your-productivity.html

Substance Abuse and Mental Health Services
     Administration, Updated October 7, 2020. Retrieved
     on October 10, 2020, from
     https://www.samhsa.gov/find-help/national-helpline

Television Habits, Encyclopedia.com, Updated October 23,
     2020. (Copyright 2020) Retrieved on October 25,
     2020, from
     https://www.encyclopedia.com/medicine/encyclopedias
     -almanacs-transcripts-and-maps/television-habits

Ten Travel Habits to Adopt Now, from Brownell. Retrieved
     on October 17, 2020, from
     https://www.brownelltravel.com/blog/travel-habits/

The 10 Bad Habits Gen-Y Has Developed from Being
     Babied by Our Parents, by Eddie Cuffin. Published
     October 28, 2013, in Elite Daily. (Copyright 2020)
     Retrieved on October 15, 2020, from
     https://www.elitedaily.com/p/7-instagram-pictures-to-
     take-in-sorority-sweatshirts-swag-38853981

The Couch Potato Guide: 11 Ways to Make YourTV Habit Healthy. Published byEveryDay Health Newsletter. (Copyright 1996-2020) Retrieved on October 21, 2020, from https://www.everydayhealth.com/healthy-living-pictures/the-couch-potato-guide-ways-to-make-your-tv-habit-healthy.aspx#:~:text=%E2%80%9CResearch%20shows%20TV%20can%20rejuvenate,a%20bust%20%E2%80%80%94%20to%20your%20health.

The Effects of Sleep Deprivation on Your body, Healthline Media, (Copyright 2005-2020). Retrieved on October 2, 2020, from https://www.healthline.com/health/sleep-deprivation/effects-on-body

The Elements of Good Judgment, by Sir Andrew Likierman, from January-February 2020 issue of Harvard Business Review, Retrieved on October 6, 2020, from https://hbr.org/2020/01/the-elements-of-good-judgment

The Orthopaedic Institute, Southern Illinois Western Kentucky. (Copyright 2020). Retrieved on October 11, 2020, from https://www.orthopaedicinstitute.com/new/the-best-and-worst-exercises-for-back-pain

The Science of Drug Use: Discussion Points, from the National Institute on Drug Abuse, Advancing Addiction Science. Published May 26, 2020. Retrieved on October 17, 2020, from https://www.medicalnewstoday.com/articles/252684

The Ten Worst Habits for Your Mental Health from Careers In Psychology. Retrieved on October 8, 2020, from https://careersinpsychology.org/ten-worst-habits-mental-health/

Top 10 Habits to Break as a Family, from All Pro Dad. Retrieved on October 16, 2020, from https://www.allprodad.com/top-10-habits-to-break-as-a-family/

Want to be Successful? Do These 7 Things in Your Spare Time, By Larry Alton, Published in Success on September 6, 2017. Retrieved on October 17, 2020, from https://bestlifeonline.com/after-work-habits-productivity/?nab=1

What is high potassium or hyperkalemia? From American Kidney Fund. Updated on July 20, 2020. Copyrighted. Retrieved on October 17, 2020, from https://www.medicalnewstoday.com/articles/252684

What's to know about gambling addiction, by TImothy J. Legg PhD., CRNP, Written by Tim Newman on June 19, 2018, in Medical News Today. Copyright 2004-2020. Retrieved on October 11, 2020, from https://www.medicalnewstoday.com/articles/15929#getting_help

Why do we need magnesium? Published in Medical News Today. Copyright 2004-2020. Retrieved on October 17, 2020, from https://bestlifeonline.com/after-work-habits-productivity/?nab=1

Why Gambling is Good for You, by Timothy Dawson, June 26, 2018, on LegitGamblingSites.com. Copyright 2015-2020. Retrieved on October 11, 2020, from https://www.legitgamblingsites.com/blog/why-gambling-is-good-for-you/

READ OTHER
BOOKS FROM CHRISTINA FANELLI

50 THINGS TO KNOW ABOUT KNITTING: KNIT, PURL, TRICKS, & SHORTCUTS (50 Things to Know Crafts)

Greater Than a Tourist - New York USA: 50 Travel Tips from a Local: Greater Than a Tourist New York

Stay up to date with new releases on Amazon:
https://amzn.to/2VPNGr7

www.ingramcontent.com/pod-product-compliance
Lightning Source LLC
Chambersburg PA
CBHW061358250726

48657CB00004B/1547